# Xenophobe's®
## guide to the
# FINNS

## Tarja Moles

Xenophobe's Guides

Published by Xenophobe's® Guides

Telephone: +44 (0)20 7733 8585
E-mail: info@xenophobes.com
Web site: www.xenophobes.com

First printed 2011
Updated/reprinted 2011, 2012, 2013, 2014

Editor – Catriona Tulloch Scott
Series Editor – Anne Tauté
Cover designer – Vicki Towers
Printer – CPI Antony Rowe, Wiltshire

ePub ISBN: 9781908120366
Mobi ISBN: 9781908120373
Print ISBN: 9781906042318

# Contents

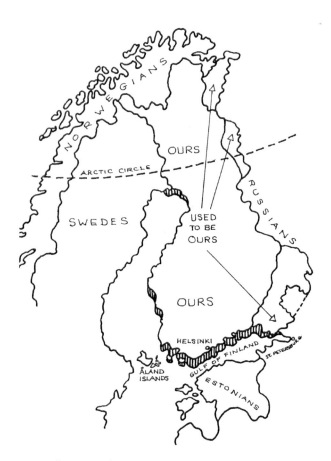

5.4 million Finns live sandwiched between 9 million Swedes and 142 million Russians. The Finns also have 77 billion trees, 187,888 lakes, 264,000 moose and 1 Santa Claus (who they claim is the genuine one).

The area that is their homeland is almost as big as Germany, and it is expanding by about the size of Gibraltar each year due to post-glacial rebound.

# Nationalism & Identity

## Forewarned

The Finns are a little different from the average Western nation. Extraordinary, some might say. Unlike most Europeans, they don't speak an Indo-European language. In fact, they hardly communicate in their own Finno-Ugric language, preferring not to squander their words. They are a gutsy, honest, hard-working, reliable, socially responsible, down-to-earth kind of people who respect others' privacy to

**66 They respect others' privacy to such an extent they avoid looking you in the eye. 99**

such an extent they avoid looking you in the eye. They share an aversion to whingeing with the Aussies, but not their social ease with strangers. They envy the Mediterranean people their climate, but do not care for their flamboyant show of emotion. A Finn can get extremely angry or ecstatically happy without the use of any facial expressions or change in tone of voice. He will only wave his hands when drowning.

## National pride

The Finns are convinced that there is no better country than Finland, which they call Suomen Tasavalta – Suomi for short. They extol the beauty of its thousands of lakes and thick forests; hills in the east, rivers weaving through pastoral land in the west and the tundra in the northern region of Lapland. They think that of all the places on the planet it is the safest place to live: there are no volcanoes, tsunamis, hurricanes, earthquakes or deadly spiders. The fact that the mercury can plunge below -40°C in winter and you can die of hypothermia if you don't dress appropriately is a minor inconvenience. The possibility of being mauled by a bear in the wilderness is also, of course, barely worth mentioning.

**❝ That you can die of hypothermia if you don't dress appropriately is a minor inconvenience. ❞**

Some Finns feel that Finland should include other bits of land, such as the part of Karelia which was lopped off the rest of Finland by the Russians after World War II (and which is the 'Karelia' of the Karelian question in Finnish politics.) Others prefer to let sleeping dogs – or more accurately, the Russian Bear – lie.

The slogan 'Swedes we are not; Russians we do not want to become; let us, then, be Finns' was coined in the 19th century and still reflects the Finns' pride in their national identity and separateness from their megalomaniac neighbours.

The Finnish flag with a blue cross on a white background represents freedom, the blue being the embodiment of the sky and the lakes, and the white symbolising clouds and snow. It is proudly hauled up flagpoles all over the land* to honour numerous official flag days, election days and private celebrations. It is also clearly printed on the packaging of products made in Finland. This is so that native shoppers immediately know which tomatoes and cucumbers are home-grown – less to indicate the absence of unnecessary food miles, more to denote the superior standard of Finnish produce.

When it's not feasible to fly the flag, it is always possible to flaunt its colours. The Finns have a collective fascination with the colour blue. Ask any

> **66 They loyally vote for their siblings at the Eurovision Song Contest, even if the Swedes do not always reciprocate. 99**

Finn what their favourite colour is and they will tell you this without a moment's hesitation. In fact, you don't even need to ask because the evidence is so clear. Just look around and you will notice that they all wear blue clothes. Admittedly, they also wear black and grey in winter, but that's only an attempt to add variety to the otherwise all-pervading blueness.

## How they see others

The Finns are part of the Nordic happy family, so much so that the largest concentration of expatriates are found in Sweden. Finns loyally vote for their siblings at the Eurovision Song Contest, even if the

---

* Though the autonomous region of Åland, a group of over 6,700 skerries and islands, hoists its own blue, yellow and red flag (and issues its own stamps).

Swedes do not always reciprocate. As all the family members would agree, the Swedes act as if they're superior to everyone else. However, the Finns have known for centuries that they are not really very brave. Having conquered Finland in the Middle Ages, the Swedes used Finnish peasants for cannon fodder in their military conflicts with

> **66 Finns feel that the Swedes lack backbone because they spend more time talking than getting things done. 99**

Russia. In 1809 in the Napoleonic wars, Sweden made fatal mistakes that resulted in Finland being handed over to the Russians. Lack of military prowess made the Swedes eventually give up their dream of northern domination, and instead, adopt pusillanimous neutrality. Hence, the jokes:

> 'What is the world's thinnest book?'
> 'Swedish war heroes.'

> 'What does the Swedish war flag look like?'
> 'A white cross on a white background.'

Basically, Finns feel that Swedes lack backbone because they are too soft, and spend more time talking, negotiating and making sure that everyone has had a chance to express their views, than getting things done. In their eyes, the majority of Swedish men are gay. The rest are shy, taciturn, reliable and willing to push a pram. This means they don't have balls. It so happens that Finnish men are also shy, taciturn and willing to push a pram.

But they are real men – men with a modern twist.

Other Westerners that really count for the Finns are the English and Americans. The non-hooligan stratum of English society with its politeness and 'stiff upper lip' represents the sort of culture many Finns idealise. And since there have been no important soccer internationals in Helsinki, the Finns still retain the illusion that most of the English are ladies and gentlemen who drink five o'clock tea and live in rose-covered cottages, or mansions in Surrey.

Finnish youth culture is heavily Americanised. However, apart from American tourists in the capital, Finns rarely see living specimens of the genus, though the great-grandchildren of Finnish settlers from the wilds of the northern US do, on occasion, visit their roots.

> **66** The Finns would be very happy if the Russians were someone else's neighbour. The Swedes, for instance, would be an ideal candidate. **99**

By contrast, Russians are seen only too often. The Finns detest their brutal eastern neighbour who bullied them for over a century before conceding their independence in 1917. A Finnish author once observed that the fundamental problem with Russia is its location. The Finns would be very happy if the Russians were someone else's neighbour. The Swedes, for instance, would be an ideal candidate. Judging by the several attempts to make it happen, Moscow seems to have been of exactly the same opinion.

The Finns are convinced that Russia still has its eye on their country and could attack at any time, like it did during World War II, when it annexed bits of Finland. However, Moscow knows that the Finns are no pushovers. Of all the countries that Stalin wanted to take over, Finland was the only one that kicked up a fuss, did a lot of damage to the Russian troops (Molotov cocktails were developed by the Finns), and ultimately, did not lose its independence. Nowadays the Russians seem to have introduced a more cunning plan to take over the country: their nouveaux riches have started to buy the land, piece by piece, supposedly for use as holiday resorts.

**66 The presence of the Russians on the roads has also introduced a new form of the old game of Russian roulette. 99**

Russian lorries and imported cars abuse the Finnish roads by using Finnish ports to siphon goods from Western Europe. You can tell when a car transporter has docked. Shiny black Mercedes, all with tinted windows, form extended convoys across southern Finland as they head towards the eastern border at breakneck speed. The presence of the Russians on the roads has also introduced a new form of the old game of Russian roulette: you no longer need to possess a gun to have a one-in-six chance of being killed.

The Finns are linguistically related to the Estonians. There is a brotherly feeling towards them, the Finns being the superior big brother in this instance. Estonia is the only foreign country where the Finns can be understood in their mother tongue. Add to this Estonia's low prices and you can see why the country is like one great theme park for Finnish shopaholics, cosmetic surgery tourists and old age pensioners having spa holidays. Most importantly, the proximity of Estonia to Finland makes the Finns look more respectable: booze cruises to Tallinn contribute to reducing the official alcohol consumption figures, making the nation look more sober than it actually is.

> **"Estonia is like one great theme park for Finnish shopaholics, cosmetic surgery tourists and old age pensioners having spa holidays."**

## How others see them

They don't. Well, apart from the Estonians (and to a lesser extent, the Swedes) who see a fair number of Finns staggering off the Baltic ferries – not because of seasickness but because they have already started sampling the bounty of the floating tax-free liquor stores. On land, they rapidly empty the local shops of beers and spirits, pausing only to drink the nearby pubs dry. Then they return to the ferries on their hands and knees, dragging purposely designed booze trolleys behind them. It is not difficult to see why the

Finns, given their giant physique and inebriated elegance, have earned themselves the Estonian nickname 'moose'.

To the Swedes, the Finns are inscrutable and enigmatic. Other than this, they seem to be pretty much off the planet's radar. The world media occasionally mention Finland's welfare state, high living standards and motor racing successes, but these are soon erased from the international collective consciousness. Vague ideas about saunas, snow and blonde women persist. The rest of the information is often muddled up. Hence, every Finn acts as if employed by the Finnish Tourist Board and unwearyingly keeps on putting the facts straight, especially these:

> **66 Every Finn acts as if employed by the Finnish Tourist Board and unwearyingly keeps on putting the facts straight. 99**

1. Nokia is not a Japanese mobile phone giant. It shares its name with a small town in the western region of Finland, where it originated. Before making phones mobile, the company was busy making people mobile – via the manufacture of tyres and rubber boots.

2. The Finns are not like the Swedes. They are better than the Swedes.

3. Santa Claus comes from Finland. Full stop.

## How they see themselves

Despite their small number, the Finns see themselves as a nation embracing a wide range of distinctly separate tribes, each having its own dialect, local culture and character traits. Linguistic differences between regions are so great that Finns regularly fail to understand each other.

Tavastians in Central Finland are said to be quintessentially Finnish. They are salt-of-the-earth kind of people, reticent, stubborn, trustworthy, serious, pragmatic and strong. Their speech is laconic and they are slow to get their words out. They are also slow to embrace change and slow to act. In fact, slow in every sense of the word.

> **66 Linguistic differences between regions are so great that Finns regularly fail to understand each other. 99**

Ostrobothnians in the west are the biggest show-offs. For centuries they were known for their vigour, explosive tempers and predisposition to using a *puukko*, a sheath-knife, to settle disagreements. If there weren't any *puukko* fights and at least one death at a wedding, it wasn't worth getting dressed up for. Thanks to the Ostrobothnians, Finnish surgeons are considered world-class in vascular reconstruction.

Karelians in the south-east are the liveliest of the Finns. They are chatty, friendly, spontaneous and musical. Their dialect is frequently made fun of by other Finns because it makes them sound dim-witted. They like their food and have the best culinary repertoire in the country. The only loss of life at a Karelian wedding would arise from someone choking on a piece of smoked fish because they had been attempting to eat, laugh, talk and sing at the same time.

Savonians in the east have the gift of the gab. They are cheeky, witty and playful in a laid-back kind of way. They frequently use sayings, riddles, euphemisms and roundabout ways of expressing themselves. As it is impossible to get a straight answer to a question, the listener has to assume responsibility for the interpretation. And unless you're a Savonian, it is not a win-win situation.

> **❝ As it is impossible to get a straight answer to a question, the listener has to assume responsibility for the interpretation. ❞**

*Finlandssvenskar* – as the Finland-Swedes call themselves – are a Swedish-speaking minority, making up 5.5% of the population. They inhabit the coastal areas and the archipelago in the south-west where they sail, compete in team handball, play folk music in village fiddle groups and dance around the maypole at Midsummer. Of all Finns, they are the most sociable and community-orienated. Marrying one is like marrying a Finnish ice hockey player: you will be sharing your life not just with your spouse but with the rest of the team.

Then there are the residents of Lapland in the far north. They are known for their excessive appetite for reindeer meat, alcohol and sex. Considering the environment in which they live – the Arctic night lasting up to a couple of months – you can hardly blame them. What would you do after the novelty of watching the northern lights has worn off?

# Obsessions

## Navel gazing

The Finns are very self-critical and spend a good deal of time gazing at their navels, both individually and as a nation. Collectively, they are obsessed with how others see them and constantly strive to polish the 'Suomi-kuva', the 'Finnish image'. Sports, business, technology, peace negotiations, science, education, design, safety, basically anything that will show their country in a positive light is promoted. Every foreign news programme, article and YouTube clip is scrutinised to see what is being said about Finland. Which is not a lot most of the time. But when there is something, the Finnish media spends more time covering the foreign report than the actual news.

**❝ The Finns are very self-critical and spend a good deal of time gazing at their navels. ❞**

Their obsession is summed up in this tall story:

A Frenchman, a German and a Finn were in Africa and came across an elephant. The Frenchman looked at the creature and straightaway started thinking about the variety of culinary delights he could cook from it. The German pondered the animal's potential as a vehicle on the savannah and how its performance compared to that of his Jeep. The Finn's immediate thought was: 'I wonder what the elephant thinks of me?'

Finns would love to be noticed by other nations. It never ceases to amaze them that the Americans don't know where their country is, let alone the name of its capital. Admittedly, there are situations when it's perhaps not that bad to remain in relative obscurity: every time the Russians have set their eyes on Finland, it's caused nothing but trouble.

## Outdoing the Swedes

The Finns and the Swedes share the same values and coexist very amicably. Until they start competing with each other. It doesn't matter whether it's about the excellence of their particular welfare societies, the superiority of their respective mobile phone technologies or international rankings in ice-cream consumption, the Finns will always want to beat the Swedes. The competitiveness between the two nations is particularly fierce in the field of sports. Each summer they meet eye to eye in the Finland-Sweden Athletics International, the only annual bilateral sports event in the world. Although few world records have been broken in these competitions, they are extremely prestigious and extraordinarily intense, so much so that it's not unheard of for athletes to resort to punch-ups in order to prevent the runner in the next lane reaching the finishing line first.

Even in international competitions the Finns measure themselves against the Swedes. Winning is, of course, great, but beating the Swedes is even better. The Finns never tire of exulting about their victories in the 1995 and 2011 Ice Hockey World Championships, which were particularly sweet due to having beaten Sweden into second place. These were such major events that the nation overcame its reclusiveness and

> **❝ It doesn't matter whether it's about the excellence of their welfare societies or international rankings in ice-cream consumption, the Finns will always want to beat the Swedes. ❞**

huge crowds formed in city centres, celebrating the double triumphs. The fact that the Swedes did the same to the Finns in the 2006 Winter Olympics was not so well received. Especially since the Swedes added insult to injury by suggesting that the Finns make substitute gold medals for themselves out of tinned pineapple rings and strings of liquorice.

## The sauna

The Finns' lives revolve around the sauna (an ancient Finnish word for a steam bath/house). For over 1,500 years it was the place for births, bathing and burial preparation. Whenever the Finns built new houses, saunas were erected first. This was to ensure that people could keep warm and not die of hypothermia. Contemporary Finnish UN peacekeeping forces have continued this practice by making it their top priority to construct saunas wherever they are sent in the world. Including equatorial Africa.

**66 There are over 2 million saunas in Finland. This means that at any given moment all the population could be sitting in a sauna. 99**

There are over 2 million saunas in Finland. With a nation of 5.4 million inhabitants, this means that at any given moment all the population could be sitting in a sauna – which they do at least once a week on a Saturday evening (*saunapäivä*, 'sauna day'), if not every night.

There are private saunas in people's homes and summer cottages. There are public saunas at swimming pools, sports clubs and business premises. Even the Parliament House has its own sauna. After all, where else would you make the country's most important decisions than sitting in the sauna stark naked with your colleagues? The democratic process does not get any more egalitarian than this.

In fact, the sauna epitomises the value of equality. Everyone is the same when all is stripped away and one sweats together in extreme heat – just as nature intended, the Finns believe. They think that bathing in the sauna has a soothing effect, too. It is not just a space where you wash your body, but also where you cleanse your mind and rejuvenate your spirit.

> **In summer they take turns to beat themselves with bundles of fresh leafy birch twigs to invigorate the skin.**

In summer they sit in the sauna and beat themselves with bundles of fresh leafy birch twigs to invigorate the skin. They only stop when there are no leaves left in the bundles. Since only real sauna enthusiasts use birch bundles throughout the year – stripping the birches of their twigs in midsummer and filling their freezers with them for use in other seasons – most Finns rely on their bodies to tell them the right time to stop: just before their hearts are about to pack up.

The experience is topped off by jumping into a lake to cool down, or (in winter) lowering oneself into a hole in the ice or rolling about in the snow afterwards.

> **It's a fact of life that the Finns don't function properly if they can't bathe in the sauna regularly.**

It's a fact of life that the Finns don't function properly if they can't bathe in the sauna regularly.

Even in extraordinary situations, such as during World War II, it was fundamental that enough time was allocated for this – the soldiers' rest period was determined on the basis of the time it took to build, heat and bathe in the sauna (8 hours).

Withdrawal symptoms can be severe if access to the sauna is denied for a prolonged period of time. This can be seen most clearly at the Helsinki-Vantaa airport luggage collection point. Finns returning home from abroad are frantically ringing their families. Instead of say-

> 66 Withdrawal symptoms can be severe if access to the sauna is denied for a prolonged period of time. 99

ing, 'Hello darling, I've missed you,' they blurt out with desperation in their voices, 'Heat the sauna. I'll be home soon!'

The Finns can't quite fathom why many foreigners don't fully appreciate the relaxing effect of the sauna, but instead regard the practice as evidence that the Finns are masochists. Those unsuspecting foreigners who have undergone the experience tend to attribute the sauna's stress-relieving properties to the fact that it is not possible to think about your worries while your body is being subjected to an onslaught of flagellation and extreme temperature change. And that the biggest stress relief comes from finally getting out of the hothouse alive.

# Character

## *Sisu*

*Sisu* encapsulates the Finnish psyche. The word is not as untranslatable as the Finns would like to think – it is just that it is nice to be able to point to something which nobody else has. It is a mixture of stamina, doggedness, tenacity, stubbornness, what you will, but it means first and foremost that Finns don't give up at the first hurdle. It is *sisu* that makes the Finns sit on the ice jigging for fish in -20°C though they could just go to the super-market. It is *sisu* that has them

> **❝ *Sisu* means first and foremost that Finns don't give up at the first hurdle. ❞**

picking wild blueberries in a forest for days on end without so much as a flinch when clouds of mosqui-toes feast on them. Foreigners – mostly from the Far East or students from the former Eastern Bloc – can only be persuaded to do the same with the incentive of earning some cash by selling their take to berry processing companies.

It is *sisu* that prevents the Finns from calling for help when they get stuck waist deep in a swamp during their hiking holiday in Lapland. Instead, they will casually tread the sludge and retain their relaxed facial expressions until they have freed themselves eight hours later. Then they will finish the remaining 20 kilometres they had set out to do that day.

*Sisu* is an introverted strength. It is about being stoical and not complaining. If something has been started, regardless of whether it's important or sensible, it has to be finished. Whatever must be done will be done, no matter what it takes.

> **If something has been started, regardless of whether it's important or sensible, it has to be finished.**

Matti is a case in point. He decides to pass a rainy day relaxing in the sauna at his *mökki* (summer cottage). He will use birch wood in the stove as this makes the heat delightfully intense. Arriving after a 6-hour car journey, he admires the neat piles of chopped wood in his shed, but cannot spot a single piece of birch. He contemplates heating the sauna with what he's got, but quickly discards the idea. Instead, he picks up an axe, goes out in the torrential rain, fells a birch tree in the nearby forest, chops it, takes the pieces to the sauna and, reaching into his pocket for his matches finds they are now soaked.

He drives 50 kilometres to the nearest petrol station and buys ten packets. Back in the sauna he tries to kindle the birch, but the wood is simply too wet. Now more determined than ever to use birch, he gets in his car again. Five hours and seven hardware stores later, he returns. 'This time it's going to work and nothing will stop me from having a relaxing day,' he swears, as he gets out of the car with his new blowtorch.

Finnish *sisu* has developed over thousands of years.

It has been a struggle just to survive in such a remote location and hostile climate. Quite apart from resisting military domination and linguistic and cultural influences from their neighbours, the Finns have had to battle against freezing temperatures, turn swamps into arable land by sheer hard work and hoes, and wrestle with bears.

Modern technology has made it easier to survive in Finland, but global warming has not yet made a noticeable difference to its severe winters. *Sisu* is still

> **66** *Sisu* **is still very necessary if you want to perform a simple task such as drive to work on a winter's morning. 99**

very necessary if you want to perform a simple task such as drive to work on a winter's morning. Provided it's not below -30°C (in which case you walk because the tyres would split if you attempted to drive on them), you go outside, take a guess as to where your 18-year-old son might have parked your car the night before, start shovelling to find the car, continue to dig the car out of the snow, and finally, scrape the thick and stubborn layer of ice off the windows. If you are lucky, this will only take you 45 minutes, and it will turn out to be your car rather than your neighbour's.

After several attempts and some moderate swearing, your car starts. Just as you are ready to move off, the snow plough goes past creating a metre-high wall between you and the road in a matter of seconds. Out comes the shovel again.

When you finally make it to the office two hours later – but still in time, of course (the Finns are never late) – a colleague asks if you had any difficulties getting to work. You reply: 'Not really.'

## Competitiveness

The Finns are extremely competitive, albeit in a modest kind of way. They constantly measure themselves against other nations. Deep down in every Finn there lurks a fear that others consider them country bumpkins. After all, Finland remained an agrarian society until as late as the 1950s. So international competitions and rankings of all kinds are taken as opportunities to show how rapidly and effectively Finnish society has developed and how the Finns have become a truly sophisticated nation. The ultimate evidence is, of course, the civilised behaviour of Finnish tourists abroad: unlike some other nations, who get heavily drunk, become loud and shame their compatriots by being a right nuisance, the Finns only get heavily drunk, fall in the gutter on their way to the hotel and stay there quietly and without disturbing anyone until the first rays of the sun shine wake them from their stupor the following morning.

> **Deep down in every Finn there lurks a fear that others consider them country bumpkins.**

The competitive streak in the Finns is also a manifestation of the nation's pent-up *sisu*. As the ease of modern life threatens to make it redundant, the Finns have needed to channel it into something else. Finland has become the promised land of competitions.

There are events for swamp football, wife-carrying, throwing mobile phones or milking stools, playing the air guitar, chain-saw sculpturing, dog sledging, reindeer racing, playing football with slippers on and the Lappish biathlon where you alternate between skiing and

> **When it comes to competing, Finnish imagination knows no limits.**

lassoing reindeer… When it comes to competing, Finnish imagination knows no limits. Someone even organised a championship event for killing mosquitoes which was held inside a tent full of the insects – until the animal rights groups intervened and it had to be stopped.

One contest that typifies the Finnish mentality is the Sauna World Championship. The competitors sit in 110°C heat while water is poured on the stove every 30 seconds to make sure that no-one can complain of being cold. The last person to stagger out of the sauna unaided and vaguely lucid is the winner. So far, Finnish men have never been beaten by other nationalities. This has been put down to *sisu*. *Sisu*, and the frequent practice the men get every time they take a sauna together and tacitly compete against each other, despite denying that they do.

The Finns are particularly competitive in sports, and even more so if the sport requires true grit. All Finnish children are conditioned to compete from an early age. Those who are 'born with skates on' are taken to ice hockey training sessions before they can walk. Those who haven't been so fortunate are bought a pair of skis and egged on to go round and round the ski track in dark and frozen pine forests. By the time they start school they will have won numerous trophies in children's cross-country skiing competitions. In most other countries making children race across country that is still inhabited by wolves in icy temperatures would result in the intervention of social services. Not so in Finland. This is merely an initiation into being a Finn; a means of preparing for the annual Finlandia Ski Marathon. Even if you never take part.

> **❝ The Finns are particularly competitive in sports, and even more so if the sport requires true grit. ❞**

Although competing is important, winning is even more so. If you're a Finnish Olympic champion you may even be given land and have a house built on it for you by your local community. The Finns have never got their heads round the British notion of giving their best but not really worrying about the end result. Why send Eddie 'The Eagle' Edwards to repre- sent the UK in Olympic ski jumping when he was so bad that the International Olympic Committee had to modify its rules to prevent anyone like him ever participating again? Why compete if you are only going to embarrass yourself? If your best is not enough, you just have to try harder.

## Reticence

The Finns are the ultimate quiet types. Some would go even as far as to say they are autistic. 'Talking is silver, being silent is gold' is a Finnish maxim. Being competitive, they will aim for the gold.

As with *sisu*, Finnish reticence has been borne out of the harsh climate and geographical isolation from the rest of the world, and, in the sparsely populated hinterland, even from each other.

Considering the nation's uncommunicativeness, it seems surprising that mobile phones have become so popular: 98% of the Finns own at least one. Apart

> 66 'Talking is silver, being silent is gold' is a Finnish maxim. Being competitive, they will aim for the gold. 99

from being a patriotic duty to support the national brand, they help the Finns retain their large personal space. It's bad enough to have to go shopping when there are three other people in the supermarket.

The Finnish economy with words has also been noted in the foreign media. Former Formula 1 champion Mika Häkkinen became famous for his monosyllabic answers to lengthy questions posed by international journalists. At least the journalists got a reply from him; not all Finnish drivers have been so verbose.

> **Finnish melancholy can be so extreme that other nations might classify it as depression.**

When you compare the Finns with other nations, it may seem that they are all introverts. However, this is not the case. There is a simple test which gives away an extrovert Finn: when he is talking to you, he looks at your feet instead of his own.

## Melancholy

Many nations claim to be melancholy. There is something beautiful about it when it implies soulfulness. But Finnish melancholy is something quite different. It can be so extreme that other nations might classify it as depression, citing Finland's high ranking in the Western world's suicide statistics as proof.

Naturally, it is easier to get depressed in winter when the sun hardly rises above the horizon. Long winters with their inevitable ice, snow and darkness have spawned Finnish poems such as:

> A winter bridge frost
> darkness,
> as if the world
> ends at the parapet.

But, come the summer and the Finns are like a different species: in cities, café terraces are filled with tentative smiling faces and stiff tongues are loosened by the outrageously expensive Finnish beer and cider; in the countryside, friends, relatives and business partners get together in summer cottages for sauna and skinny-dipping. Everyone enjoys the latest flavours of Finnish ice-cream and strawberries grown under the midnight sun. The young become so animated that they head off to heavy metal music festivals instead of listening to their CDs on their own; the older generation dance the tango cheek to cheek on open-air dance floors. Jollity is tangible. If it weren't for the blue clothes, you would think that aliens have taken over the whole nation.

> ❝ Come the summer and the Finns are like a different species. ❞

## The State & Society

The Finns live in a technologically advanced information society. Automated means of doing things are the norm and only 4% of the population are still resisting the lure of a broadband connection. You can access public services online and travel on trains without drivers. You can have your cows looked after by a mechanised system which washes and milks them whenever they care for a break from chewing the cud. You can even have all your post delivered to your electronic mailbox, provided you don't mind someone opening and scanning your love letters and reminders to attend your next colonoscopy appointment.

There is a high expectation that everything in Finland functions efficiently. Public transport, health care, emergency services, rubbish collection and all other services just happen, as if no-one put in any effort. It's really only the annual national rash of strikes organised by various labour unions demanding higher pay that have the potential to disrupt the smoothness of everyday life. The Finns do not, however, fight at the barricades as fervently or as frequently as the French. Their obedience to authority and community-oriented way of thinking make them feel guilty about disadvantaging the rest of society. Besides, when so many people come together to support one cause, it's just too uncomfortable to stay at the crowded barricades for long and it becomes really difficult to avoid making eye contact.

> 66 Their community-oriented way of thinking makes them feel guilty about disadvantaging the rest of society. 99

## Education
In Finland, the early years of childhood are considered precious. Children only start school when they are

seven, and even then they have shorter school days, longer holidays and less homework than most other Western pupils. You would think that this would make the Finns a bunch of ignoramuses but according to the Programme for International Student Assessment (PISA), the Finnish system produces teenagers who are among the smartest in the world. Furthermore, they're well-rounded in a variety of subjects ranging from sciences to arts. It is not uncommon for pupils to be able to read a music score by the time the 9-year compulsory schooling finishes.

These achievements have been attributed to highly-qualified teachers, a relaxed learning environment and the equality principle which dictates that gifted and weak pupils are not separated, and the former help the latter if they have finished their own work.

> **66 The Finnish system of education produces the world's smartest teenagers. 99**

As plausible as these reasons sound, they do not take into account an additional factor: the positive impact of the wintry weather. If you are chucked outdoors for a quarter of an hour every 45 minutes, you're more likely to sit still at your desk when you come back inside – not only because your mind is refreshed, but because your body is too frozen for you to do anything else.

The excellence of education is not limited to schools; the Finns think their vocational schools, colleges, polytechnics and universities are also first-class. Qualifications, and the pieces of paper on which these are written, are important in Finnish society. It is the thoroughness that comes from rejecting multi-tasking and adopting a single-minded focus on doing one thing at a time that makes Finnish degrees so superior. Finns reckon this is proved by the fact that it takes Finnish students longer than most others to graduate.

## The nanny state

The Finns' attitude to authority has been shaped by a long history of being forced to obey foreign rulers unquestioningly. The nation remains obedient and has a great respect for the State, the all-pervading power-house that nannies the people, keeps its beady eye on them and dictates what's good for them and what isn't. This is the way the Finns like it. Even if they grumble about it. After all, the State is always there to pick up the pieces if your health fails, if you lose your job, or if the speed of your broadband connection falls below your legal right to enjoy at least 1 megabit per second.

> **The State is keen to protect its citizens from all harm, including their own vices.**

The State is keen to protect its citizens from all harm, including their own vices. It ensures that the nation won't drink itself to extinction by monopolising the sale of all strong alcohol through its Alko shops. Additionally, every drop of booze is so heavily taxed that there will always be enough cash in the coffers to fund any liver transplant that may be required. Provided, of course, that you had sufficient funds to get yourself into such a pickle in the first place.

High taxation of cigarettes, the prohibition of smoking in public spaces and the tobacco advertising ban are aimed at helping the nation breathe only pure clean air. Anti-drink-driving laws and recommendations for cyclists to put on helmets and for pedestrians to wear reflectors on their clothes are designed to ensure that no-one is injured on the roads.

> **❝ In other countries the label 'a nanny state' is a pejorative term. In Finland it's a compliment. ❞**

Even bullying at school is reduced by rules dictating what kinds of names parents are allowed to give their offspring. Forget about naming your child after his or her place of conception or your favourite foreign pop star, and embrace good old Finnish names that can be easily pronounced by everyone, such as Jyrki, Väinö or Kaija-Marjatta.

In other countries the label 'a nanny state' is a pejorative term. In Finland it's a compliment. It means one can sleep soundly at night, knowing that the State will look after everyone's well-being and the greater good of the whole country. Micro-management is not only deemed necessary, it is welcomed by the citizens.

Even if they are among the most educated people on the planet, it would not do to trust the Finns to make the right choices.

## ID cards

Some nations see ID cards as a threat to liberty and privacy. The Finns embrace their personal numbers as a convenient way of reducing red tape. For example, proving your identity is much easier. Instead of showing photographic evidence of who you are and providing utility bills to confirm where you live, you can just present your number. Informing everyone of your change of address is straightforward. You don't have to write to your bank, tax office, vehicle licensing agency, insurance providers and so forth, separately. You simply fill in one electronic form and the Population Register Centre will notify all the relevant parties automatically.

> **66 The Finns embrace their personal numbers as a convenient way of reducing red tape. 99**

Unfortunately, occasional administrative errors are also transferred across the system at the press of a button. Before you know it, you might find yourself in a Catch-22 situation: how do you prove you are still alive when the system clearly says you are dead and has already automatically annulled your magazine subscriptions along with your pension?

## National Service

Hunting is a Finnish tradition, so the handling of guns is no novelty to many young Finns in the countryside. By the time the Finnish Defence Forces invite 18-year-old able-bodied males to a 6-12-month mandatory adventure camp (females have the option to take part), these novices are already sharpshooters. They would have obtained their hunting firearms licences at the age of 15 (pending safety checks and parental permission) and practised on targets such as moose, bears, foxes, hares, ducks and geese as often as these licences allowed (the number and type of wildlife being strictly regulated).

> **66 Hunting is a Finnish tradition, so the handling of guns is no novelty to many young Finns. 99**

Military service is seen as an important patriotic duty. It also has a great impact on your future life, not only because you have to attend refresher exercises every so often, but because it can help you to get a job. Employers are more likely to appoint someone who has done well during their service than a conscientious objector who has opted to push pensioners around the park instead. Nor should you underestimate the transferable skills acquired during your service. Surviving the wilderness exercises boosts your *sisu*, and learning to do what you are told and not minding the absurdity of the commands enables you to endure an incompetent boss in your workplace.

Knowing how to make a bed is guaranteed to dramatically decrease the number of arguments you may have with your wife. Not that everything is prescribed in the Finnish military: you are still free to squeeze the toothpaste tube in any way you wish.

## Crime and punishment

Finland does not have as many police officers as most countries since it is the people's own consciences that do most of the policing. Parents don't slap their children because the State would prosecute them. Shoppers don't taste the grapes in the supermarket before buying them because it would be considered theft of a most serious kind. Pedestrians don't cross an empty street if the red man is showing – not even if it's 3 am on a winter's morning, -20°C, and there is no car, let alone another soul, in sight.

> **❝ It is the people's own consciences that do most of the policing. ❞**

The crime rate in Finland is one of the lowest in Europe. No-one clutches their purses when shopping or hides their possessions from sight in parked cars. It always surprises the Finns when they are robbed on holidays abroad. For how are you supposed to know that someone might steal your belongings if you leave your bags unattended in the hotel lobby while nipping into the toilet?

There is one crime, however, that appears to be irresistible. And it pops up just before Christmas. Every Finn has been imbued with the idea that if Santa Claus sees you doing something wrong especially before Christmas, there will be no presents. Yet this threat has no effect when it comes to Christmas tree poaching. The Finns widely believe that the most beautiful Christmas tree is one that they've seen in a forest that is not public property. The illicit and daring nature of the escapade only fuels their desire for the forbidden. Poachers particularly favour those that are growing in State-owned woodland. The City of Helsinki has now introduced a made-to-measure fining system for each metre of stolen spruce.

The Finns hold the view that loss of freedom is a major punishment. Finnish courts impose exceptionally short

> **66 Finnish courts impose exceptionally short sentences and try their hardest not to send anyone to prison. 99**

sentences and try their hardest not to send anyone to prison. The Court of Appeal in Eastern Finland is particularly famous for its leniency towards rapists: the quickness of the act and the importance of the rapist's permanent job have both been cited as reasons for mitigating the District Courts' original punishment. However, commit a crime against the State, like fraud or tax evasion, and you'll suffer for the rest of your life.

# Attitudes & Values

## The influence of religion

The Swedes started converting the Finns to Catholicism from the 11th century onwards, while the Russian Orthodox Church attempted to convince the heathen nation that its version of Christianity was the correct one. The Finns' worship of the high god *Ukko*, sacred animals and other deities was gradually wiped out, and it was Lutheranism in the 16th century that ultimately won the Finnish soul. The values of

> **66 The values of hard work and humility found a receptive ground in the Finnish psyche. 99**

hard work and humility found receptive ground in the Finnish psyche. The possibility of an afterlife in heaven, instead of the inevitability of going to the underground land of the dead called *Tuonela*, as the Finnish pagan beliefs had it, was reasonably attractive. The most persuasive argument for conversion was, in reality, the compulsion to belong. Compulsion at the point of a soldier's sword, you understand, not by choice.

Nowadays nearly 80% of the population are members of the Lutheran Church. However, the majority of this pragmatic nation sees its affiliation, and the consequent state-administered payment of church taxes, as an investment for having christenings, confirmations, weddings and funerals in a church.

Occasionally, to get their money's worth, they might even attend a Christmas service.

Although only a small minority is actively involved in the church or one of its revival movements, the whole population still carries the legacy of Lutheran values on its shoulders. The biblical dictum, 'By the sweat of your brow you will eat your food until you return to the ground', is still very much adhered to.

You would think that because life is as tough as it is, you would not have to make it even harder. But no, the Finns revel in hardship. They are at their best when circumstances are at their worst. And when things aren't so bad, it's important to give others the impression that they are.

> **The Finns revel in hardship. They are at their best when circumstances are at their worst.**

Take Pekka as an example. His business is going well and the future looks promising. He owns a lovely house and has a beautiful wife and well-behaved children. You pay an innocent compliment and congratulate him on how well he has done for himself. Pekka quickly starts finding fault: the business is not really doing that well and he was just very lucky to have survived the recession; the house is just a kit house and wasn't actually built by him; his children are bound to stop behaving well once they reach their teens, and his wife, well, she is sure to go off with someone else because he still hasn't got round to building the *mökki* by a lake that he promised her ten years ago.

The Finns' instinct is to think that good things cannot come easily and that, if and when they do, they cannot last. Other nationalities feel guilty when, by commission or omission, they have done something wrong and failed. The Finns feel guilty when they have done something right and been successful. Their strong sense of humility dictates that you must neither brag about your accomplishments nor celebrate them.

One can anticipate a desperate job interview scenario, for how do you know what different candidates are capable of if they habitually put themselves down? The trick is that both the interviewer and the interviewee are Finns. They have a mutual understanding of what everything means. The interviewer knows that 'basic French' is equivalent to having studied the language up to degree level and spent three summers in Paris on additional language courses in nanotechnology, the cultures of pre-colonial francophone Africa and other useful specialist vocabulary. Things only get complicated when foreigners apply for jobs. For instance, when an American asserts that his French is conversational the Finns are initially very impressed, only to discover later that the American is referring to the fact that he did indeed once have a conversation with an attractive French lady in France – in English.

> **66 The State works hard at treating all its citizens in the same way. 99**

## Equality

The concept of equality forms the basis of the Finnish welfare society. The State works hard at treating all its citizens in the same way. Everyone receives the same State schooling where they are forced to eat the same nutritionally-balanced school dinners, served on identical plates and eaten with identical knives and forks.

They then move on to further studies where they earn the right to put healthy refectory food on their plates themselves. On getting a job, they continue eating subsidised wholesome meals at the

> **66 The Finns were the first Europeans to liberate their men from the burden of governing the country without the benefit of female guidance. 99**

workplace canteen. It's only after they retire that they are trusted to decide for themselves what to eat for lunch. That is, until they are admitted to a retirement home where they will once again be fed institutionally-prepared food, though now from spoons or through a tube. All identical, of course.

The Finns were the first Europeans to liberate their men from the burden of governing the country without the benefit of female guidance. Finnish women have been able to vote and stand for parliament since 1906, longer than any other European country. Since then, the male Finn's obligation to provide exclusively for his family, pay when on a date and open doors for women has also been removed. Women have stepped into the public sphere, making Finland the most gender-balanced country in the world. There have been two female Prime Ministers and one President. Women occupy more than 40% of the parliamentary seats, the younger ones publicly breast-feeding their babies while arguing for better services for families with children. The men are spending more time at home changing nappies, thanks to the provision of generous paternity leave.

The principle of equality has also been observed in the establishment of a classless welfare society. Free education, almost free healthcare, a generous benefits system and a better state pension than elsewhere, guarantee equal opportunities for all citizens. The only problem is that all these require a considerable amount of public revenue. This is why the common assertion that to be born in Finland is like winning the jackpot in the lottery is only applicable when you are at the receiving end of these services. A far more common experience is that you need to win the lottery just to cover the tax bill.

> 66 Finnish honesty is about meaning every word that comes out of your mouth. 99

## Honesty

In Finland honesty is not just the best policy, it is the only policy. The Finns are among the least corrupt and most transparent nations in the world. If they say they will do something, they will keep their word. The only mitigating factor for not fulfilling a promise is death. And even that is considered a poor excuse.

Finnish honesty is about meaning every word that comes out of your mouth. This is why you have to give the Finns time to think through what it is exactly that they want to say. Honesty is also responsible for their bluntness: At a diplomatic dinner, a Finnish Ambassador was seated next to an American lady who said: 'Mr Ambassador, I have taken a bet that I can get you to speak more than five words this evening.' After a lengthy pause the Finn replied: 'You lose.'

## Practicality

If the principle of equality is the cornerstone of Finnish society, the principle of practicality is the way in which the rest of the house is built. Homes are super-insulated and triple-glazed. This keeps the indoors at tropical tempera- tures so that it's quite pleasant to go outdoors every once in a while to cool down.

Venetian blinds are put between the window panes so you rarely have to dust them.

> **66 Homes are super-insulated and triple-glazed. It's quite pleasant to go outdoors every once in a while to cool down. 99**

Plate racks are fitted in cupboards above the kitchen sink so that you never have to dry the dishes. Not that you need these now that there are dishwashers, but it's practical to have them nonetheless: you never know when you might need to hide empty bottles at short notice. Or, if you're a student, require a place for growing cannabis.

> **❝Conditions are so good that large numbers of bears, moose and wolves sneak across the border from Russia. ❞**

Finns have never been slaves to fashion trends – practicality and comfort always outweigh any aesthetic considerations. For instance, in winter the need to wear multiple layers of clothes makes you resemble the Michelin man (to the degree that handshakes on leave-taking have to be completed before donning one's heavy-duty outdoor garments). In spring and autumn it's best to encase yourself in a shell suit. And in summer, white tennis socks with sandals are second to none at preventing mosquitoes from biting your ankles. If you are sceptical, see how long you will last without them.

## Being green

Two-thirds of Finland is covered in forests, Finland's 'green gold' which provides the raw material for one of its most important export items – paper. It's a natural environment that provides a haven for wild-life. All non-game birds and mammals are protected and as hunting is carefully regulated, the conditions are so good that large numbers of bears, moose and wolves sneak across the 1300km-long border from Russia to start a new life as ecological migrants.

The Finns are eco-conscious and generate less household waste than the European average. This stems from efficient recycling and constant media reinforcement. The deposit scheme for glass and plastic bottles rewards environmentally-friendly behaviour. The biggest queues at Alko shops are not for buying wine, but for returning bottles. Even children know that collecting the empties during and after music festivals can take them a step closer to attaining a new iPod with relatively little effort. Less eco-fanatic citizens have been persuaded to sort their paper from their bio-waste and to wash their empty Tetra Paks: the threat of fines always works wonders in Finland.

> **❝ Another form of recycling is the Finnish tradition of finding inventive ways of reusing things. ❞**

Another form of recycling is the Finnish tradition of finding inventive ways of reusing things. You can crochet plastic bags into rugs for your *mökki*'s outhouse. You can freeze berries in empty milk cartons and use old tyres as raised beds for flowers. As early as 1974 Finland's most widely circulated magazine, *Pirkka*, started publishing readers' *niksit* (hints and tips). It spread the gospel of life-enhancement through the discovery of new uses for mundane objects. The nation was hungry to learn how you could make glue by mixing vinegar and gelatine leaves. Or mend a hole in your umbrella with a sticking plaster.

The uses for pantihose have kept many readers enthralled. Initially, recommended for such unexciting purposes as storing onions in the garage or making shoelaces from long strips, suggestions now range from pulling them over your head as you are about to go on a roller-coaster to prevent your spectacles from falling off during the ride, to a solution for a comfortable night's sleep on a long-haul flight – tying yourself to the back of your seat with a Rambo-style headband so that your head doesn't flop down when you nod off.

> **66 The uses for pantihose have kept many readers enthralled. 99**

# Manners & Mores

## No small talk

The Finns don't see the point of small talk. Why say anything if there is nothing worthwhile to say? If you start a conversation on the weather, the Finns will think that you really want to talk about it. If you ask 'How are you?', it will be considered a genuine enquiry, not a synonym for 'Hello'.

In the rest of the world, conversation follows the rules of ping-pong. Interruptions are common and keep the discussion on-going. For Finns, conversation resembles bowling. Everyone patiently waits his turn and interrupting another speaker is considered impolite. Finns are better at listening than at talking. Jorma Etto, a Finnish author and poet, described them as a people who don't answer when asked, who answer when not asked, and who ask when there is no-one to answer. Not exactly a definition of a perfect conversationalist.

Making small talk is not simply a Finnish aversion. It's a national handicap. They cannot do it to save their lives. This is clear from the way they behave when going berry and mushroom picking in the forest. To deter any bears from coming close you need to make some noise. A group of people of any other nationality would have a good old chinwag amongst themselves. The Finns strap bands with jingle bells around their wrists.

> **Making small talk is not simply a Finnish aversion. It's a national handicap.**

## Keeping it curt

Finns are courteous when it matters. 'Sorry' is reserved for more serious offences than accidentally bumping into someone in the street. In fact, it's almost impossible even so much as to brush against anyone's arm unintentionally. Because everyone is so cautious about keeping their physical distance from each other, such a situation always comes as a great surprise to the Finns. You can observe their bewildered facial expressions as they blurt out: 'O-hoh' (Oops).

Exchanges in shops are curt. You are not considered rude if you simply state the name of the item required. No 'please' (there is no such word in Finnish), and no 'thank you'. In winter, when it's -20°C and you've nipped out wearing only a jumper, you don't want to waste time, or have your teeth crack with sudden changes in mouth temperature. And in summer, succinctness prevents you getting a mouthful of mosquitoes.

Not holding a door open for the person following you is not discourteous. It's a way of avoiding unnecessary interaction. Not asking your work colleague 'How're you?' is not impolite. It's being respectful of his or her privacy. After all, no-one likes a busybody. Not offering to help or give unsolicited advice is not rude, but an indication that you don't wish to interfere in other people's affairs. However, if you ever do ask for help, people will take it seriously and make your problem theirs. They won't rest until the matter is resolved and you have been helped so much that you wish you had never asked.

> **66 In summer, succinctness prevents you getting a mouthful of mosquitoes. 99**

## Compliments

The Finns become more than ordinarily tongue-tied when it comes to paying compliments. Indeed, it would not even occur to the Finns that they could analyse something to an extent that would warrant the use of two sentences of praise.

Flattery is deeply discomforting for the Finns. Foreigners who innocently admire them, or things Finnish, are viewed with suspicion. So the best way to express approbation is to keep it terse and understated. This will indicate to a Finn that you have already settled in well and begun thinking like a Finn.

## Swearing

What the Finns lack in the quantity of their speech, they make up for in its potency. A liberal sprinkling of swearwords is not only a must for achieving street-cred, it's the key to effective communication.

There is an ample assortment of profanities to choose from, ranging from the biblical to anatomical to scatological. *Vittu* (fuck, cunt) is undoubtedly the

> **What the Finns lack in the quantity of their speech, they make up for in its potency.**

most commonly used, especially among the young. Weaving several different swearwords into one sentence can add significant intensity to the underlying meaning. For instance, the statement *juhlissa ei tarjottu viinaa* (there was no booze available at the party) is totally inadequate in describing the disappointment of the situation. Add a few extra words and the frustration becomes apparent: *vittu siellä helvetin juhlissa mitään saatanan viinaa tarjottu jumalauta* (fuck, there was no Satan's booze available at Hell's party goddammit).

Finnish swearwords are so powerful that Finns often modify them to dilute their impact, or use foreign words which, to them, don't have such a strong edge. The English words fuck, hell and shit as well as the German *Scheisse* (shit) are commonly used since their potency level is roughly on a par with the expression 'Oh poo!' At least to the Finnish ear.

> **66 Finnish swearwords are so powerful that Finns often modify them to dilute their impact. 99**

The father of all swearwords, originally the name of the god of thunder and later used to denote the devil in the Bible, is *perkele* (the emphasis is on the 'r': *peRRRRRRRRRkele*). If you ever need to express your dissatisfaction in very strong terms, no other word will do.

## Punctuality

The Finns' unforgiving attitude to lateness is founded on common courtesy which demands that you must not keep people waiting. If the Finns are exactly on time, you will know there have been complications; otherwise they would have been there well in advance. They even turn up at the bus stop 20 minutes before the bus is due. You might think this is unnecessary, but try arriving just a few minutes before the designated

> **66 They even turn up at the bus stop 20 minutes before the bus is due. 99**

time and you will find that the bus has already gone. Bus drivers also follow the maxim of not keeping people waiting.

## Greetings

Finns feel no need to overdo a greeting. Kissing on the cheek is considered pretentious and is embarrassing. '*Hei*' or '*hej*' (hello) does nicely or the more formal '*hyvää päivää*' or '*goddag*' (good day), depending on one's language group.

However, if you are meeting someone for the first time, you have to shake hands. Briefly. This also applies if you haven't met someone for a long time. If you are close, you might even give them a hug. But all hugs should be quick and awkward.

## Hospitality

The guest-host etiquette is full of unwritten rules that ensure that both sides look generous and appreciative of each others' efforts. An invitation to someone's home or *mökki* means bringing something – a packet of coffee (if that's all you're invited for), chocolates or flowers. You take your shoes off as you enter (the Finns like their homes clean and will most likely have sterilised their parquet floors for your visit). You will then be taken to the sitting room. No drink will be offered at this stage. The Finns eat and drink at the table and the time in the sitting room is for conversation – as difficult as this may be.

> **66 The Finns like their homes clean and will most likely have sterilised their parquet floors for your visit. 99**

When you are invited to the dinner table, you say 'thank you', but continue sitting. When invited for the second time, you do the same. At the third bidding you go, but hesitantly so as not to look too eager. The table will be loaded with so much food that its legs look ready to collapse under the strain. Try to dismiss the thought that it will soon be your legs that have to bear the weight.

At the table, guests are expected to serve themselves. This is because whatever you take, you must also eat – a fact that does not mean you can select what you like. Etiquette demands that you take a little bit of everything, even if you don't normally eat vegetables and there are seven varieties on offer. The hosts will wait for you to start, but you mustn't dive in as this will make you look as if you've only come round for the food. Again, a hesitant manner is required.

It needs to be kept in mind that guests have to have a second helping, so it's wise not to scoff too much during the first round. Even when the hostess notices that you are full – the give-away sign being food pouring out of your ears – she will continue to press you to more. It is entirely in order to keep declining politely. There is no point in secretly calling the family dog to your rescue because he will have struggled with his own plateful and won't be interested in yours.

> 66 Finnish hospitality is akin to feeding the guests to death. An invitation for 'just a coffee' is never just that. 99

Finnish hospitality is akin to feeding the guests to death. An invitation for 'just a coffee' is never just that. It will be accompanied by a selection of cinnamon buns, cakes, pastries and biscuits. If you don't taste them all, you are seen as snooty, as if the spread was not good enough. You will also be obliged to drink several cups of coffee. As soon as your cup is empty, it will be filled well before you are able to open your mouth to say, 'No, thanks'. And if the hostess doesn't think you are drinking your coffee quickly enough, she will top up your cup anyway. Any protests to stop the coffee coming your way won't work until you have had at least two refills. Since it's considered extremely rude to leave anything, there is no escape.

The best strategy for surviving Finnish hospitality is not to accept too many invitations in the same week.

# Behaviour

## The battle of the sexes

There are no real incentives to being married in Finland: cohabiting is socially acceptable, there are no married couples' tax allowances and the divorce legislation makes gold-digging impossible.

Unlike in some countries where the women have at least let the men entertain the idea of being in charge, there have been no such concessions for Finnish men. Even the most macho men have been turned into *tohvelisankarit* (henpecked husbands; literally, heroes in slippers) the minute the vows have been exchanged. As one writer noted, 'Finland is a potential paradise for stressed males who hate to make decisions. Here you can just lean back and let yourself sink into the lap of an intelligent woman equipped with loads of will-power.' The Finnish woman will not only decide what her mate should think and say, she will even pull his socks up for him. However, having a dedicated personal life organiser to fill the void following completion of National Service may now be short-lived since the divorce rate has reached 50%.

The Finns think that, ultimately, their compatriots make the best spouses. They share the same values,

> **❝Even the most macho men have been turned into *tohvelisankarit* (henpecked husbands; literally, heroes in slippers).❞**

are reliable and don't need to tell each other several times a day that they love each other. Finnish men are frequently the butt of unkind remarks. They are accused of being depressed, taciturn, and consequently, unromantic. This is unfair because it is possible to find a Finnish man who is cheerful and communicative and who gives presents. His name is Santa Claus.

## Family matters

Childhood is associated with nostalgia in Finland. And with costliness. Due to the country's extreme climate, parents need to kit their offspring for all kinds of weather, not to mention acquiring the equipment for every seasonal hobby, be it a bicycle, ice hockey gear, skis or snorkels. And this is before the kids are old enough to demand their own computer games because their dads won't let them have their turn.

> **It would be too expensive to have children in Finland if the State did not lend a hand.**

It would be too expensive to have children in Finland if the State did not lend a hand. Every family is entitled to generous child benefits. Paid parental leave can be taken either by the mother or the father until the little one reaches the age of three. Every expectant mother receives a free 'maternity pack' which is a cardboard cot full of essential – and eco-friendly – baby paraphernalia: summer and winter clothes, toiletries, bedding, reusable nappies, toys and the all-important instruction manual of how to operate the baby. Free health clinics look after the next generation's health and inject them with all the possible vaccinations. Activity clubs and toddler groups stimulate their early social development. Special daytime child-friendly cinemas are propitious environments for the parents to interact with each other, thereby enhancing their well-being. Some rural towns and villages attract families by offering free land to households with children. A parent pushing a pram travels free on public transport in the Greater Helsinki area since parents couldn't possibly be expected to direct their attention to such a trivial matter as paying the fare when they have the future of the nation to look after.

> **Some rural towns and villages attract families in order to boost their population by offering free land to households with children.**

Finnish babies are acclimatised to the weather conditions from the very beginning. They are wrapped in layers and layers of thickly-insulated clothes and duvets and put into prams to have their nap in the open air in winter. Letting youngsters go out in the autumn without hats or gloves on would be considered an act of gross neglect. The parents' obsessive mindset regarding keeping children warm does not wane on the hottest of summer days, either: taking off excessive layers is only contemplated just before the infant is about to pass out from heat exhaustion.

In Finland there is no such thing as bad weather, only bad clothing. Thus toddlers and older children are made to play outside regardless of whether it rains or shines. In the face of any resistance, parents are quick to tell them that they are not made of sugar, so won't dissolve even though the rain is so hard that it's likely to damage the roof. Just put your waterproofs and rubber boots on and off you go. Schoolchildren, however, are not forced out during their breaks if the temperature falls below -30°C. The only catch is that school thermometers seem to have a special kind of mercury that never drops that low, even though you were sure that it was -40°C when you left home.

> **In Finland there is no such thing as bad weather, only bad clothing.**

In the same way as dogs are taught to come to you when their name is called, it is important for Finnish parents to teach their offspring to do the same. This is because all Finnish children look identical in their snow suits, with only their chubby cheeks and button noses showing. If they don't come when called, the parents are in danger of taking the wrong child home from the playground. Fortunately, this is not a big deal – you can always swap them over the following day.

## Eccentricity

The Finns embrace eccentricity whole-heartedly. This may sound like a contradiction in terms considering the importance they place on not standing out in a crowd. However, when the entire nation is eccentric, it's easy to conform.

> **66 The Finns are well aware that they are bit a unusual. They are proud of it. 99**

There have been numerous peculiar fixations that have swept the country. For example, in the 1990s there was the craze for wearing *antennipipo*, crocheted skullcaps with an antenna-like appendage on top. Why? Because they looked funny. By the end of the 20th century it was not just competitive skiers and demented grannies who walked about in summer with ski poles in their hands but no skis attached to their feet; it had turned into the fashion for Nordic walking.

The Finns are well aware that they are a bit unusual. They are proud of it. If you live in a village, one of the highest honours you can achieve is to be called a village fool. Not because it would indicate that you're a simpleton, but because the term is used in some places as a way of recognising your value in, and your contribution to, your local community.

## Driving

Finland is renowned for its Formula 1 and rally drivers: Häkkinen, Räikkönen, Kovalainen, Rosberg,

Salo, Kankkunen, Vatanen, Mäkinen, Grönholm, Alén. 'If you need to win, you need a Finn' has become a common proverb in motor-sport. Foreigners have attributed the Finns' astonishing success to the environment and the nation's mentality. Finns learn to drive on dirt roads and ice – as opposed to tarmac and speed bumps – as soon as they are tall enough to reach the pedals. In their early teens they borrow their dads' farm vehicles and old bangers and race on potato fields or frozen lakes. By the time they get their driving licences they have already acquired the elemental Finnish character trait of being suicidal so necessary to negotiating the twisting rural roads at breakneck speed. *Sisu* gives them the edge in competitions by rendering them calm and determined under pressure (i.e. when facing death).

Drivers have to be prepared for the unexpected. The State has spent millions creating underpasses for Finland's moose whose minds may be engaged elsewhere, particularly in the

> **66** *Sisu* **gives them the edge in competitions by rendering them calm and determined under pressure (i.e. when facing death). 99**

rutting season. Moose come second only to alcohol as the biggest cause of road accidents in Finland.

All these factors undoubtedly play a role in producing vigilant, speedy drivers, but there is an even more fundamental reason for Finnish success. Over the years the Darwinian principle of '*Heikot sortuu elon tiellä, jätkät senkun porskuttaa*' (The weak fall down during the journey of life, the tough just keep on going) has done its job: those who weren't capable of driving winding icy roads in the darkness at maximum speed and dodging the moose have simply been eliminated by natural selection.

# Sense of Humour

It is only the inadvertent twitching of the corners of their eyes and mouths that expose the Finns' internal mirth. Expressionless Finnish faces have puzzled many visiting comedians who have initially assumed that their acts have been failures, only to find glowing comments in the press the next day.

Finnish humour is witty, dry, sardonic, cheeky and self-deprecating. They love situational comedy and wordplay. Except for jokes about the Swedes. With those, it doesn't matter how lame the joke is, it is still hilarious, e.g:

'Why don't the Swedes drink tea?'

'Because the teabags would get stuck in their throats.'

The opportunity for a sharp barb is rarely missed: Esko and Paavo are talking about the speeches they have given during their election campaign. 'What did you say?' asked Esko. 'Nothing.' 'I know that, but what words did you use?'

They excel in exaggerating their own stereotypical behaviour, such as their reticence (e.g: Two Finns pass each other in the street. One murmurs, 'Nice day!' The other replies, 'No need to make a big song and dance about it.'), or the fact that alcohol plays such a significant role in their lives:

Here is a good game for Finns that can be played on two levels: regular and advanced.

Regular: Three Finns go into the sauna, each with half a litre of Kossu (Finland's famous Koskenkorva vodka). They drink the vodka, and then one man goes outside. The other two have to guess who went outside...

Advanced: Two Finns go into the sauna, each with a litre of Kossu. They drink the vodka, and then one goes outside. The other one has to guess who went outside.

Yet another dominant topic is their *sisu* and stoicism, aptly illustrated by this joke:

It is 1939 and two Finnish foot soldiers are pinned down in a battle during the war between Finland and Russia. 'We're outnumbered,' one soldier says. 'There must be over forty of them and only two of us.' 'Dear God,' exclaims the other, 'It'll take us all day to bury them!'

# Leisure & Pleasure

The Finns' leisure activities are determined by seasonal changes. In winter it's easy to lie dormant on your sofa and watch TV. However, numerous evening classes attempt to prevent the nation's spiral into a state of somnolence by the teaching of new skills, like belly dancing, ice art, changing your car tyres or making shopping bags from used coffee packaging. Learning a new language is common, too, as many wish to improve their communications with foreigners both at work and during their winter holidays in the sun. As a consequence, most Finns are fluently silent in several languages.

> **66 Numerous evening classes attempt to prevent the nation's spiral into a state of somnolence by the teaching of new skills. 99**

When the snow begins to thaw, the citizens no longer feel bogged down by the weight of winter. Frenzied summer activities start as the bipolar nation is taken over by the manic phase. It frolics from the annual Housing Fair to the Kaustinen Folk Music Festival to the Savonlinna Opera Festival. It checks out the latest cinema art at the Midnight Sun Film Festival in Lapland before hiking the 80-kilometre *Karhunkierros* (Bear's Ring) trail in Kuusamo in the north-east. Ballroom dancing techniques that were acquired at evening courses are put into practice at the annual *Tangomarkkinat*, the world's oldest Tango

Festival. Of course, by the time the participants have lubricated themselves enough to overcome their intrinsic shyness, it doesn't really make any difference whether they have learned to tango during the winter or not.

> 66 Whereas the tango has become Finnish in spite of itself, it is when Finns dance the *humppa* that they are most truly in their element. 99

Whereas the tango has become Finnish in spite of itself, it is when Finns dance the *humppa* that they are most truly in their element. The *humppa* is a quick-step waltz. The way in which *humppa* dancers stamp and whirl around the dance floor seems to combine Finnish peasant origins of previous centuries with a secret urge to show off, to compensate for the cold, the snow, the distances and the isolation. There is not a little *sisu* in the Saturday night fever of the Finns.

## Sports

Seasonal changes do not affect the Finns' love of sports. They are eager to watch them on TV any time of the year. As for actually doing it themselves, walking, cycling and swimming are the most popular. In summer the south-western archipelago is a magnet for Finnish and Swedish tourists, so much so that hundreds of kilometres of tarmac roads have been crammed onto the myriad of islets. In winter, Finns are not satisfied with peddling on a stationary exercise cycle, splashing about in a swimming pool or practising golf indoors. Instead, they buy studded winter tyres for their bikes, swim in freezing lakes, and tee off on 'whites' (fairways of ice).

Ski-jumping and ice hockey are obsessions (though *pesäpallo*, Finnish baseball, is the national game), and Finns have a special affinity with cross country skiing. When Finland fought the Winter War against the Russians in 1939-40, the men who were called for service in the front line had to bring their own underwear, their own boots and their own cross country skis. No-one doubted they had them.

## Back to nature

The Finns' love and respect for nature is such that most family names are formed of words taken from the natural environment, such as Stream, Lake, Forest, Stone, Birch, Pine, Bear and Woodpecker. Fascination with Mother Earth and the Great Outdoors stems from most people having grown up in not-so-urban environments, even if they are currently living in cities. (Not that the cities are that big in any case: Helsinki proper is the largest and it has fewer than 600,000 inhabitants.)

**66 Most family names are formed of words taken from the natural environment such as Stream, Lake, Stone. 99**

Many long to return to their roots and regain the freedom of their childhood and wild youth. The older generations reminisce about how they used to ice-skate on the lakes, jump on haystacks in barns during the hay-making season, and exchange their first kiss behind the milk churns. The fact that they also had to help their parents dig stones out of the fields, milk the cows by hand at five o'clock in the morning and ski 10 kilometres to school in the darkness of freezing winter months doesn't seem to diminish their nostalgia. Even if it means travelling 1,100 kilometres from Helsinki to, say, northern Lapland and back again in a weekend, the few hours at the log cabin in the midst of fresh-smelling pine trees, the sun shining throughout the night and the feeling of space when no-one else is around far outweigh the minor aggravations of a total travel time of 28 hours and the vicious bites of the Lappish mosquito.

> **A few hours at the log cabin far outweigh a total travel time of 28 hours and the vicious bites of the Lappish mosquito.**

The Finns believe that it is everyone's fundamental right to be allowed to roam freely and free of charge in the countryside, in forests and on lakeshores without the landowners' permission. This belief has been crystallised into the so-called Everyman's Rights. Provided you don't cause any damage and disturb other people and wildlife, you may use the natural environment as your gym, hotel and pantry.

Hikers in the wilderness also have access to little wooden cabins (with a circle of stones for barbecues), which are maintained by the State-run forest administration as shelter for skiers in winter and for ramblers in summer. Should you arrive at one that is already fully occupied, the person who has stayed there longest is obliged to move on.

# Eating & Drinking

The Finns like to have at least two hot meals a day. If they also decide to stuff themselves with oat porridge on rising and before going to bed, this adds up to four. Live through the Finnish winter and your body craves hot food from tip to toe. It also craves comfort food.

> **Live through the Finnish winter and your body craves for hot food from tip to toe.**

Though people eat pretty much what other Western nations eat, distinctive Finnish tastes have by no means disappeared. Breakfast consists of tea or coffee, buns or crispbread, cheese and cold meats, and occasionally *viili/fil*. *Viili* is a yogurty substance with the consistency of stretchy jelly. In the olden days, when it came in wooden pails as opposed to plastic pots, you were provided with a pair of scissors to detach your portion from the rest.

Rye bread and glassfuls of cold milk form an integral part of every meal, so you can have your Big Mac with a sour-rye bun and wash it down with milk.

Even doner kebabs are served with special chilli sauce made to suit the bland Finnish palate, namely, without the chillies.

> **66 Karelian stew (a hearty, two-meat casserole), meatballs and sautéed reindeer shavings are enjoyed throughout the year. 99**

Seasonal produce is a big thing in Finland: the nation thinks that all food should be eaten when it's at its freshest. So, it's new potatoes with herring in early summer, wild berries in late summer, crayfish in August, and forest mushrooms and game in autumn.

Fine dining also reflects this. When the French President dined with the Finnish President, the menu comprised morel and willow grouse soup, terrine of arctic char and cold smoked grayling, reindeer fawn, and a souffle of Finnish honey, lingonberries and ice-cream.

The right time for having sausages and beer is always after the sauna, and meat pasties taste best on the way home from a night club. Thursday is customarily the day for pea soup and oven pancakes. Karelian stew (a hearty, two-meat casserole), meatballs and sautéed reindeer shavings are enjoyed throughout the year. So, even in winter, is ice-cream. Foreigners frequently wonder why the Finns would subject themselves to eating something cold in winter, but the Finns understand that sacrifices have to be made in order to maintain their ranking as the No. 1 ice-cream consumers in Europe (14 litres per person per year). *Salmiakki,* salt liquorice (which gets its distinctive flavour from a mineral found in volcanic rock), is a Finnish passion. The Finns are so enthusiastic about the stuff they have founded the Salt Liquorice Association whose members keep in touch with each other through Facebook.

> **The Finns like to do everything early rather than risk being late, and mealtimes are no exception.**

It isn't enough just to enjoy *salmiakki* on its own, the more gastronomically inclined buy *salmiakki*-flavoured pork chops or prepare their own *salmiakki* marinade for the grilling season. The argument about the superiority of *salmiakki* over chocolate and vice versa no longer exists as the two have been merged into one – a *salmiakki* chocolate bar. And s*almiakki* ice-cream washed down with *salmiakki* vodka now constitutes the young Finns' Friday night supper.

## Getting a head start

The Finns like to do everything early rather than risk being late, and mealtimes are no exception. By the time Mediterranean people have stirred from slumber, the Finns have consumed their morning porridge or open sandwiches plus a cup of coffee before going to work, had another coffee and possibly a cinnamon bun on arrival and eaten a refectory lunch even as early as 10.30 am. Afternoon coffee with more cinnamon buns and cakes is at 1pm. Between 4.30pm and 6pm they will have dinner, and at about 8pm indulge in a light supper to ward off any night-time hunger pangs.

## Coffee

In coffee consumption the Finns lead the world. Each person has around 9 cups a day. What is more, although only lightly roasted, traditional Finnish coffee is so concentrated that a spoon will stand upright in the cup. You are not considered a grown-up until you start drinking coffee. Indeed, the substance is so essential

> **66 Although only lightly roasted, traditional Finnish coffee is so concentrated that a spoon will stand upright in the cup. 99**

to the Finnish way of life that people are prepared to rise above their aversion to crowded supermarkets if coffee is on special offer.

## Kippis!

The Finns say '*Kippis!*' ('Cheers!') when they raise their glasses. Or bottles, as the case may be. Their idea of social drinking is not like that of the French or Spanish, where you sip good-quality wine in a sophisticated manner while having a meal. Social drinking in Finland means getting thoroughly legless, so alcohol is merely a means of achieving a brief state of bliss. The Finns think that the stronger and cheaper the alcohol, the better. Beer cannot therefore really be classified as alcohol. The fact that it can be bought outside the Alko shops in a supermarket further proves it: the State would never let everyone get their hands so easily on something intoxicating. It's just a thirst-quencher after a hard day's work.

> **66 The Finns think that the stronger and cheaper the alcohol, the better. 99**

# Health & Hygiene

In the 1970s the Finns were one of the unhealthiest nations on earth. Their lifestyle incorporated practically every imaginable risk factor for heart disease. To prevent the nation from becoming extinct, the State initiated massive public health campaigns. It got the people moving in the great outdoors, on skis, on blades and on foot. It made the domestic food industry produce healthy food. In the 1990s the Benecol products were invented to unclog the nation's arteries. Even today you'd be hard-pressed to find any full-fat dairy products in supermarkets.

The Finns, being ever so compliant, readily embraced the changes. As a consequence, they waved good-bye to cardiovascular diseases as the leading cause of death... and welcomed alcohol as the new number one. Surely, you can't be expected to eat only rabbits' food, jog for two hours every day and not toast your achievements?

These days natural remedies are viewed with a degree of suspicion, but this has not always been the case. For example, centuries before the invention of

> **66 Centuries before the invention of Viagra the people of Lapland were using reindeer antler powder. 99**

Viagra the people of Lapland were using reindeer antler powder to help out men whose stiffness was limited to their behaviour. If you are tempted to try this remedy, you should note that it is very potent. Don't overdose as you may find yourself completely hard all the way up to your neck. Don't make a brew out of it, either. The concoction will ruin your teapot by straightening its curved spout.

## Gum for gums and tums

The nation's gnashers were another target of national public health campaigns. The use of xylitol, a natural sweetener made of birch sap and a by-product of Finland's paper industry, remains a singular feature of daily dental care: after every meal the adults' faces are contorted by the resolute mastication of xylitol chewing gum, and the children's cheeks are hollowed by the intense sucking of xylitol tablets.

The only downside of xylitol is its laxative effects if consumed excessively. As 20% of the population have lactose intolerance and consequently suffer from runny tummies, the addition of xylitol in their diets is not ideal, even though the dairy industry produces all sorts of lactose-free dairy products in an attempt to eliminate some of the nation's diarrhoea. Perhaps this is the real reason why every Finnish toilet, including the public ones, has a hand-shower beside it.

> **66 As 20% of the population suffer from runny tummies, the addition of xylitol in their diets is not ideal. 99**

## Prevention is better than cure

For whatever ailment, a visit to your local polyclinic will prompt the GP to give you an impromptu, thorough, going-over. The Finns regard this as a good thing. One wouldn't want to discover something sinister when it's too late. Most importantly, you wouldn't want to risk experiencing the Finnish health professionals' pain management techniques: namely, their reliance on the patients' *sisu*, rather than providing adequate medication.

## Being clean

The Finns don't think it's possible to get properly clean without sweating in the sauna. Even public swimming pools have strict hygiene rules: first you wash your feet with an anti-bacterial solution, next you shower and scrub yourself with soap, go to the sauna to sweat off more dirt, wash yourself again, and only then are you sufficiently clean to be allowed to plunge into the swimming pool. When you return you repeat the procedure, without forgetting the importance of thoroughly washing your swimming suit. It explains why wild swimming is so popular in Finland: it's quicker to dig a hole in the ice than go through the swimming pool hygiene regime.

**66 It's quicker to dig a hole in the ice than go through the swimming pool hygiene regime. 99**

Finnish homes epitomise the nation's obsession with cleanliness. They favour wooden floors and anti-allergenic rugs which they dutifully take outside at least once a week and hang on purposely-designed metal frames. Then they give them a good spanking. They also air their bed linen to let the freezing weather kill off the dust mites. As a result, Finnish homes are squeaky clean – and everyone is allergic to something because no-one has developed any resistance.

# Custom & Tradition

## Spring celebrations

All national celebration days in Finland are legitimate excuses to get intoxicated. Easter is the most sober of them, due to its strong religious undertones and the

> **66 All national celebration days in Finland are legitimate excuses to get intoxicated. 99**

Alko shops being closed for four full days. People spend the long weekend eating roast lamb and *mämmi*, Finnish Easter pudding made from water and sweetened rye malt – akin to a dark brown, thick porridge, which few but Finns can appreciate.

It is only the pagan-influenced customs that lighten the mood at Easter. Children collect willow twigs and brighten them with coloured ribbons, tissue paper and feathers. Then they dress up as witches and visit their relatives and neighbours. As soon as the door is opened, Finnish children start thwacking the adults with their decorated twigs, reciting poems for good luck while they're at it – a benefit that will only mate-rialise if they are given chocolate eggs.

*Vappu* on 1 May, is a carnival style festivity that marks the arrival of the spring. On the eve of *vappu* (Walburgis Night), people celebrate in city centres with white college-graduation caps on their heads, streamers around their necks, balloons in one hand

and a glass of sparkling wine or homemade mead in the other. A picnic is held the following day with potato salad, sausages, doughnuts and deep-fried pastries, sitting in a park on wet grass.

## Midsummer

*Juhannus*, or the Midsummer festival, witnesses a mass exodus of city-dwellers to their summer cottages to party around a bonfire at a lakeside or by the sea. This celebration of the 'nightless night' is enjoyed so much that it takes longer than usual to recover. (The fact that most people take their summer holidays straight after *juhannus* may not be unconnected.) Some

> **❝ The 'nightless night' is enjoyed so much that it takes longer than usual to recover. ❞**

never recover. These tend to be men who decide to do a little rowing around the lake and who invariably get the urge to stand up and pee. They are usually found drowned the following day, with their zips open.

## Winter

Then come the dark days when the Finn will first go on a brief trip round Lapland to admire the *ruska*, i.e. the golds and russets of the dying leaves, before setting off to lie for a fortnight on the beach in Torremolinos, and to drink the same red wine that is available in the restaurant back home, but at a quarter of the price.

A big occasion is Independence Day on 6 December. Finns take their independence seriously. They place two blue-and-white candles in each window and watch the President's Independence Reception on TV. The programme lasts for hours, and mostly consists of the 'VIPs' in Finnish society shaking hands with the President. Although absolutely nothing noteworthy happens, it's the most popular programme of the year.

> **❝ Finns take their independence seriously. They place two blue-and-white candles in each window and watch the President's Reception on TV. ❞**

Christmas Eve is the climax of Finnish Yuletide. The nation bathes in the sauna in preparation for a Christmas dinner of ham, gravlax, potatoes and various stews made of carrots, swede and liver – followed by rice pudding. Later in the evening the children have to sing to a visiting 'Santa Claus' for their presents.

The Finnish Santa originates from the pagan harvest festival where a man used to dress up as a fertility figure in a costume consisting of horns, a mask made of birch bark and a sheepskin jacket turned inside out. As recently as the early 1980s it was usual for Santa Claus to take this form. The Finnish word for Santa Claus reflects this tradition: *joulupukki* – a Yule goat.

New Year is marked by fireworks. While other nations raise their glasses at the sound of the clock chiming midnight, many Finns will already have raised so many glasses that they are unaware of the change of the year.

# Culture

Over half of the Finnish population regularly borrow books from public libraries. This attests not only to their love of books, but also to Finland's exorbitant book prices. Newspapers are hungrily consumed at every breakfast table. It's important to brace yourself for the day in the office and should you find yourself in a situation where communication cannot be avoided, you will have something worthwhile to say.

*Kalevala* (The Land of Kaleva) is Finland's national epic. It's a 19th century poetry collection based on Karelian and Finnish mythology and oral tradition, with all the ingredients of a great story: shamanistic journeys, unrequited love, magical singing that is more powerful in battle than violence, slavery, the creation of a machine that brings fortunes to its owners, instructions for brewing beer, impregnation by consumption of a lingonberry and, of course, several suicides.

**❝ The Finnish Santa originates from the pagan harvest festival where a man used to dress up as a fertility figure. ❞**

*Kalevala* was compiled by Elias Lönnrot who made eleven trips around Eastern Finland over a 15-year period to record ancient folklore. A multi-faceted man, who also worked as a tailor and doctor, hard work made him revel in his time off, so he became known for his affairs and jovial over-indulgence in drink – until he decided to sober up and establish the first Finnish temperance society, the Clearheads' Club. His inclusion of beer brewing instructions in *Kalevala* was rather better received than his Club.

> **Lönnrot's inclusion of beer brewing instructions in *Kalevala* was rather better received than his Club.**

Though *Kalevala* has inspired many foreign fantasy writers, including J.R.R. Tolkien, the most famous Finnish literary characters are perhaps Tove Jansson's Moomins – melancholy white trolls that resemble hippos walking on two legs – who live Bohemian lives and ponder the ways of the world as they go about their adventures in Moomin Valley.

Finnish children grow up with the Moomins' profound wisdom. It encourages them to be aware that you only live once, it advocates going back to nature and it warns that owning things only leads to worries, and suitcases that you have to drag about with you. It also gives advice on how to distinguish between good and bad people: 'people who eat pancakes with jam can't be altogether dangerous.'

## Music

Much of Finnish music has melancholy undertones. Sibelius' compositions reflect the nation's indomitable spirit and their suffering under Russian rule. 'Sorrow is the source of singing', Lönnrot wrote 150 years ago, and this is still true of current music trends: the more miserable the melody and lyrics, the better the sales.

Not surprisingly, Finland has become the Mecca for heavy metal and hard rock fans around the world. There are numerous bands to choose from, such as Nightwish, HIM, Children of Bodom. Even a group of classically-trained cellists called Apocalyptica play hard rock bare-chested in leather trousers, their long hair rhythmically whipping the air. The only Finnish entry ever to have won the Eurovision Song Contest was Lordi in 2006. This band of monsters, known for their hazardous pyrotechnics, not only beat the Swedish entry, but got an admission of their superiority from their neighbours in the form of 12 points. Not a bad day for the Finns.

> **66 The more miserable the melody and lyrics, the better the sales. 99**

Many of the older generation are great fans of tango music – not so much the Argentine tango, but the Finnish variation. Argentine tangos are much too cheerful for the Finns who prefer their tangos in minor keys and with lyrics of crushed hopes and longing for an unattainable land of happiness.

Music in Finland is not entirely gloomy. Exceptions can be found among the *iskelmät*, light popular songs. If you happen to get hold of any of the 1970s' 'Finnhits' albums, you will notice that these compilations by different artists include several jolly tunes. This is because many of the songs are not, in fact, Finnish in origin: they are Finnish renditions of international hits.

## Architecture

Most Finnish buildings were constructed following World War II. Alvar Aalto's works are the best known, though it is said that Finland has 'more great architects of the status of Alvar Aalto in relation to population than any other country in the world'. Aalto's Finlandia Hall, Helsinki's most prestigious concert venue, is typical of the Finns' fascination with asymmetrical forms and functionalism. Like the Italian Pendolino trains that the State introduced in Finland almost two decades ago, the Italian marble slabs covering the exterior of the building are unable to cope with Finnish winters. Rather than finding an alternative, it is considered perfectly acceptable by the authorities to spend taxpayers' money on financing

> 66 Finland has more great architects of the status of Alvar Aalto in relation to population than any other country in the world. 99

76

the replacement of new slabs and to keep mending the endlessly faulty trains.

At the other end of the architectural spectrum are the suburban concrete blocks of flats, which sit in clusters around cities – built rapidly and without any aesthetic considerations. Their focal point is the *ostari*, a small shopping area consisting of the most essential services: a couple of shops, bank, burger kiosk and pub. The largest, and luckiest, *ostari*s even have an Alko shop. Despite their bleak exteriors, the quality of the flats' interiors and their commutable locations guarantee their enduring popularity and high prices. The most sought-after properties in Finland are traditional red-painted wooden detached family homes with a potato patch. The nation dreams about owning a house with no neighbours nearby, yet close to shops and services, ideally in the middle of Helsinki.

> **❝ The Finns loyally buy their own designers' products – which has the effect of transforming them into design look-alikes. ❞**

## Design

Finnish design is inspired by nature, coupled with functionalism. Handmade things are highly esteemed. The Finns loyally buy their own artists' and designers' products – which has the effect of transforming the nation into Finnish design look-alikes. Luckily,

Kalevala jewellery, which borrows themes from Finnish mythology, is at hand to elevate any attire: their necklaces and earrings are more or less considered badges of patriotism, and are therefore timelessly trendy.

> **Finnish movies are a genre of their own. Few people other than Finns are capable of detecting their subtleties.**

Even the Finns' homes have an air of conformity brought about by Finnish design. They sleep between Finlayson sheets, dry themselves after the sauna with Marimekko's bright poppy towels, and sit on Aalto-inspired chairs. The centrepiece on their coffee table is the wavy Aalto vase, filled with Dutch tulips in the spring, otherwise displayed simply for itself. The kitchen cupboards are full of Iittala's glassware and Pentik's ceramics. And, of course, no home would be complete without the iconic Moomin mugs.

## Cinema

Finnish movies are a genre of their own. Few people other than Finns are capable of detecting their subtleties. Although influences from other countries, such as France, can be discerned, it's Finland's atmosphere and the nature of its people that give these movies a distinctive flavour. Often that of vodka.

The first ever Finnish feature film, made in 1907, *The Moonshiners*, was about two men secretly brewing alcohol in a forest. Things haven't moved on much since. Perhaps the most notable Finnish film director, Aki Kaurismäki, is particularly skilled in portraying these Finnish qualities. His stories focus on inarticulate, alienated and unglamorous characters in gloomy locations who stare into space for long periods of time. The actors' occasional dry-witted lines and deadpan delivery intersperse the ruminating silences. All in all, a perfect encapsulation of Finnish suburban life.

# Politics

In Finland a multitude of political parties play musical chairs and take turns at being part of a coalition government. Whichever combination makes little difference. All the parties have more or less the same views so as not to jeopardise their chances of attracting as many votes as possible from the nation that all thinks alike.

> **A multitude of political parties play musical chairs and take turns at being part of a coalition government.**

Nevertheless, there is endless bickering in Parliament. It's not a bawling free-for-all. It's a structured form of stonewalling, with one speech being read out after another, until MPs vote just to get it over with.

Finland has never had any truly colourful politicians

who would have provided juicy dramas in the tabloids. There have been attempts to rectify the dull political scene by electing celebrities such as a former Miss Finland, a singer-songwriter, a brace of skiers and a clutch of TV presenters, but the politicians' quintessentially Finnish way of dealing with the media still prevails, as summed up in this exchange:

> **"Finland's history is full of triumphs over adversity: first over climate, then the neighbours and now the international markets. "**

A Finnish diplomat was leaving an EU meeting in Brussels when a group of journalists surrounded him.

'How did the meeting go?' one reporter asked.

'No comment.'

'None whatsoever?'

'None. And don't quote me on that.'

# Business

Finland's history is full of triumphs over adversity: first over climate, then the neighbours and more recently the international markets. Finnish businesses and products have now spread around the globe and it's impossible not to come into contact with them. A Nokia mobile phone may nestle in your pocket. Your computer may be guarded against cyber-criminals by the F-Secure anti-virus and security software. KONE lifts and escalators carry you up and down. You are sure to use Finnish paper products daily, whether it's to carry your shopping in a more eco-friendly way or to wipe your behind. You may travel Finnair's shorter and faster northern route from Europe to the Far East or take a holiday on one of the world's largest cruise ships made in Finnish shipyards. Even the less techie areas of life are affected: Fiskars' tools are now more common in gardens than gnomes.

## (Un)employment

The official job centres and local Associations for the Unemployed ensure that job-seekers are fully catered for. The unemployed do not incur any costs while undertaking further education, such as courses in log-cabin building or customer service in Norwegian, or when applying for jobs (e.g. they can print their applications and use the telephone for free). Given that they can easily amuse themselves in an inexpensive way by taking advantage of cheap refectory-style lunches, concessional rates to the swimming pool and cinema, facilities for rug-weaving, and participating in free exercise classes ranging from Pilates to Zumba, there is not much incentive to actually gain employment.

> **The unemployed do not incur any costs while undertaking courses in log-cabin building or customer service in Norwegian.**

## Management by *perkele*

The Swedes have coined the term 'management by *perkele*' to portray the Finnish managerial approach. Instead of collectively pondering all the possible alternatives and letting every member of the staff from the cleaner to the MD voice their views, as the Swedes do, the Finns act swiftly and don't waste time on the decision-making process. If something isn't happening quickly enough, it is necessary for the top managers to slam their fists on the table and yell, '*Perkele!*' Repeatedly, if necessary.

> 66 The Finns act swiftly and don't waste time on the decision-making process. 99

You should not confuse this kind of behaviour with complete disrespect for consensus-based decision-making. The Finns know the precise parameters within which their responsibilities lie, therefore they expect all decision making within their remit to fall solely upon them. There is, thus, no need to ask others' opinions. It follows from this that if a manager gives someone a certain task, he or she is expected to leave the person alone to get on with the job. Any interference will be taken as criticism. Even innocent daily interest will be interpreted as a lack of trust and the manager will soon be told: 'Since you know so well how to do the job, you had better do it yourself.'

## Business etiquette tips for non-Finns

1. If a meeting is scheduled for one hour, it will last one hour. Not a minute longer. So don't divert from agenda. Meetings are for dissemination of information, not platforms for debate.
2. Don't stand or sit too close to the Finns. They need a lot of elbowroom.
3. There is no need for social chitchat before negotiations. Get down to business as soon as possible. And don't interrupt the Finns when they talk. (It's bowling, not ping-pong, remember.)
4. Understate rather than overstate your case. Finns are result-oriented people. It's your subsequent actions that the Finns will assess. 'Deeds not words' are what count.
5. Expect the Finns to follow company policies like lemmings diving off a cliff. They won't make any exceptions to the rules; nor expect them.
6. Understand that mutual agreements are there to be respected and relied on. NB: Any speculative musing on your part could be taken as a commitment.
7. If invited for a drink and sauna, don't decline. The Finns are showing their appreciation after a successful business negotiation.
8. Your standing will increase if you express an interest in Finland's sports. Fake it if you must.
9. Don't attempt to arrange meetings in the summer months. The Finns are on holiday.

# Language

It is said that Finnish is the language of heaven, not because its vowel-filled words sound divine when accompanied by the harp, but because it's so difficult to learn that you need an eternity to master it.

Rumours about 15 cases of the noun in Finnish are true enough. You stick the equivalent of prepositions on to the ends of nouns and adjectives, for example: *talo* – house; *talossa* – in the/a house, the *ssa* being the equivalent of 'in'. But it is not always that easy since, as often happens when you try to stick plastic objects together, you get a gooey mess at the join. Thus, when you want to say 'in Helsinki' you do not get Helsinkissä as you might expect; instead, the root of the word melts a little, giving Helsingissä.

> **❝ As often happens when you try to stick plastic objects together, you get a gooey mess at the join. ❞**

Finns love to put two – or more – old words together. Compound words are a challenge. For example, you might think that having to tell someone that you work in *Euroopan tilintarkastustuomioistuin* (the European Court of Auditors) is a bit of a mouthful, but try saying that you're a *lentokonesuihkuturbiinimoottoriapumekaanikkoaliupseerioppilas* (technical warrant officer trainee specialised in aircraft jet engines) in the Finnish Air Force. Even someone's name can be a trap for the unwary. One sportsman was simply known by the foreign press as 'M15' (M from his first name, and 15 indicating the number of letters in his surname).

Finns have expressions that no-one else has or can even imagine a need for. A *hanki*, for instance, is not something to blow your nose on, but a thick layer of snow which by late winter acquires an icy crust on the surface making the post-sauna roll so abrasive to the skin; *peura* denotes a wild reindeer,

> **66 Finns have expressions that no-one else has or can even imagine a need for. 99**

as opposed to *poro*, the domesticated variety; *löyly* is that special brand of searing sauna vapour. And while in many languages, the oblique points of the compass are usually compounds, such as north-east or south-west, the Finns have decided to use eight unconnected words. The word for south-west, *lounas*, is not derived from the word for west, *länsi*, nor from the word for south, *etelä*.

Finnish can have complicated constructions which means you can end up with the equivalent of: The in-the-café-sitting, bun-eating man was talking to the having-read-the-newspaper woman. Mercifully, this sort of construction is used less in speech.

Finland's brand of Swedish differs from Sweden-Swedish in the same way that American English differs from British English; the west coast Närpes dialect of Finland-Swedish is nearer to Old Norse than almost anything in the rest of mainland Scandinavia.

Swedish is Finland's second official language and the strict 'Language Law' has the country in its grip. The State administrators are obliged to serve you in either language, and it is compulsory for Finnish-speakers to study Swedish and for Swedish-speakers to study Finnish at school. The street names in bi-lingual areas also have to be in both languages, the top sign being in the language of the majority. When the Finnish-speaking municipality of Sammatti was consolidated with the adjacent bilingual town of Lohja/Lojo in 2009, the Law stipulated that the town should not only place new signs below the Finnish street names, but it would first actually need to invent Swedish names for them.

> **66 The principle of equality is reflected in the absence of genders: *hän* denotes both 'he' and 'she'. 99**

The Finnish language suits the Finnish mentality to a tee:

- The principle of equality is reflected in the absence of genders: *hän* denotes both 'he' and 'she';

- Long words ensure that there is more time to think what you want to say when you actually say it; and,

- The pronunciation style enables you to keep your face in repose because you hardly have to move your mouth.

# The Author

A former careers information officer, English teacher, youth leader and conference host, Tarja Moles now works as a freelance writer and researcher.

A native of Savonlinna (Nyslott in Swedish), Eastern Finland, she was lured into settling down in the UK after an encounter with an English dentist at the British Museum café. She warned him that she had a history of biting dentists' fingers, but he merely shrugged his shoulders, smiled and bought a pair of gauntlets.

She is a typical Finn in that she loves the sauna, misses plunging into frozen lakes and is allergic to everything. But she believes the genes for endurance sports must have skipped a generation since the game of geocaching with a GPS on Dartmoor is about as much as she can handle.

Grateful thanks are given to David Moles for his British perspective and Markku Jaakkola for his Finnish one; and to Eric Dickens and Jussi Bright for their invaluable contributions.

### The Italians

Italians grow up knowing that they have to be economical with the truth. All other Italians are, so if they didn't play the game they would be at a serious disadvantage. They have to fabricate to keep one step ahead.

### The Spanish

The Spanish voice box was originally built along the lines of a quadraphonic sound system. The result is that everyone appears to have a hearing impairment from childhood and needs to compete with others very loudly in order to be heard.

### The Canadians

Canadians wear an austere smile in the face of adversity, and have a 'grin and bear it' mentality, even if the grin is frozen on their faces by the cold. In the middle of the worst possible ice storm, someone will still manage to say: 'Well, at least there's no flies out today.'

### The Aussies

The Aussies do not wave like any other nationality. The movement they call their 'salute' is a constant hand wave in front of the face. Quite by chance this keeps the flies off their faces.

### The Americans

The American language embraces the bias towards good feelings. Stocks that plummet to half their value aren't losers, they're 'non-performers'. Someone doesn't have a near brush with death; he or she has a 'life-affirming experience'.

### The English

The English share a dislike of anyone behaving in a manner that 'goes too far'. The admired way to behave in almost all situations is to display a languid indifference. Even in affairs of the heart, it is considered unseemly to show too much enthusiasm.

Comments on Xenophobe's® Guides

## On the series:

'I own 8 of these 'Xenophobes' guides and think they're all hilarious.' Reader from Boston

## The Danes:

'This book has a wonderful energetic sense of irony and humour, combined with a deep insight into the Danish culture and mentality. The true nature of the Danes revealed!' Reader from Denmark

## The Poles:

'Entertaining, insightful and a lot of fun. According to a Polish friend, its observations about Poles are accurate. Very funny and clever little book.' Reader from Ireland

## The Spanish:

'A witty and very clever look at Spanish society. I found most of what I read to be so incredibly true that I was laughing out loud. Highly recommended.' Reader from the USA

## The Greeks:

'The author hits every part of the culture and its stereotypes with extreme accuracy. Very well written. A 'must' read.'

Reader from Greece

# Xenophobe's guides

Available as printed books and e-books:

# Xenophobe's lingo learners

Xenophobe's Guides

Xenophobe's® Guides e-books are available from Amazon, iBookstore, and other online sources, and via:

www.xenophobes.com

Xenophobe's® Guides print versions can be purchased through online retailers (Amazon, etc.) or via our web site:

www.xenophobes.com

The Publisher is pleased to offer a quantity discount on book orders. Why not embellish an occasion – a wedding goody bag, a conference or other corporate event – with our guides. Or treat yourself to a full set of the paperback edition. Ask us for details:

Xenophobe's® Guides

telephone: +44 (0)20 7733 8585
e-mail: info@xenophobes.com

Xenophobe's® Guides enhance your understanding of the people of different nations. Don't miss out – order your next Xenophobe's® Guide soon.

Xenophobe's Guides